Lovers Always

This Certifies

That on the _____ day of

_____

in the *Year of our Lord*

_____

and

_____

were by me united in
Marriage

at_____

_____

Witness

_____

_____

SMALL THINGS THAT CAN
MAKE A BIG DIFFERENCE
IN YOUR MARRIAGE

F. B. MEYER

We enjoy hearing from our readers. Please contact us at www.anekopress.com/questions-comments with any questions, comments, or suggestions.

Lovers Always
© 2022 by Aneko Press
All rights reserved. First edition 1899
Revisions copyright 2022.

Please do not reproduce, store in a retrieval system, or transmit in any form or by any means – electronic, mechanical, photocopying, recording, or otherwise, without written permission from the publisher. Please contact us via www.AnekoPress.com for reprint and translation permissions.

Scripture quotations from The Authorized (King James) Version. Rights in the Authorized Version in the United Kingdom are vested in the Crown. Reproduced by permission of the Crown's patentee, Cambridge University Press.

Cover Designer: Jonathan Lewis
Editors: Sheila Wilkinson and Ruth Clark

Aneko Press

www.anekopress.com

Aneko Press, Life Sentence Publishing, and our logos are trademarks of
Life Sentence Publishing, Inc.
203 E. Birch Street
P.O. Box 652
Abbotsford, WI 54405

RELIGION / Christian Living / Love & Marriage

Paperback ISBN: 978-1-62245-758-8
eBook ISBN: 978-1-62245-759-5

10 9 8 7 6 5 4 3 2 1

Available where books are sold

Contents

Preface: A Template for the Exchanging of Vows ix

The Wedding Day 1

The Honeymoon 7

What the Wife Expects from Her Husband 13

What the Husband Expects from His Wife 21

Difficult Marriages 29

The Home 37

The Dowry of Children 45

Common Interests 53

The Retirement Years 61

F. B. Meyer – A Short Biography 69

Other Similar Titles 73

Register This New Book

Benefits of Registering*

- ✓ FREE **replacements** of lost or damaged books
- ✓ FREE **audiobook** – *Pilgrim's Progress*, audiobook edition
- ✓ FREE information about new titles and other **freebies**

www.anekopress.com/new-book-registration

*See our website for requirements and limitations.

Preface

A Template for the Exchanging of Vows

The parts in brackets throughout may be used or not, at discretion.

The parts in italics throughout are instructions for the minister.

At the day and time appointed for the solemnization of matrimony, the persons to be married, who are qualified according to law, stand together with the man on the right hand and the woman on the left. The minister shall say, "Dearly beloved, We are gathered together here in the sight of God, and in the presence of these witnesses, to join together this man and this woman in holy matrimony; which is an honorable estate, instituted by God in the time of man's innocence, signifying to us the mystical union that exists between Christ and his church; which holy estate Christ adorned and beautified with his presence and first miracle that he wrought in Cana of Galilee, and is commended by the apostle Paul to be honorable among all men; and therefore is not to be entered into unadvisedly but reverently, discreetly, and in the fear of God.

"Into this holy estate, these two persons come now to be joined. Therefore, if anyone can show just cause why they may not lawfully be joined together, let him speak now or forever hold his peace."

[*Speaking to the persons who are to be married, the minister shall say, "I require and charge you that if either of you knows any reason that you should not be lawfully joined together in matrimony, you must confess it now. Be assured that as many as are joined together otherwise than God's Word allows are not joined together by God; neither is their marriage lawful."*]

If no such obstacle is alleged, then the minister shall say to the man, "_____, *will you have this woman to be your wedded wife, to live together after God's ordinance of holy matrimony? Will you love her, comfort her, honor and keep her in sickness and in health? And forsaking all others, will you keep her as long as you both shall live?"*

The man shall answer, "I will."

Then the minister shall say to the woman, "_____, *will you have this man to be your wedded husband, to live together after God's ordinance of holy matrimony? Will you love, honor, and keep him in sickness and in health? And forsaking all others, will you keep him as long as you both shall live?"*

The woman shall answer, "I will."

[*Then the minister shall guide the man with his right*

hand to take the woman by her right hand and instruct him to say after him as follows:

"I _____, take you _____, to be my wedded wife, to have and to hold, from this day forward, for better, for worse, for richer, for poorer, in sickness and in health, to love and to cherish, till death us do part, according to God's holy ordinance: And thereto I pledge you my faith."

Then the woman with her right hand will hold the man by his right hand and likewise say after the minister,

"I _____, take you _____, to be my wedded husband, to have and to hold, from this day forward, for better, for worse, for richer, for poorer, in sickness and in health, to love and to cherish, till death us do part, according to God's holy ordinance: And thereto I pledge you my faith."]

Then shall the minister pray thus: "Oh, eternal God, Creator and Preserver of all mankind, Giver of all spiritual grace, the Author of everlasting life, send your blessing upon your servants, this man and this woman, whom we bless in your name. That as Isaac and Rebecca lived faithfully together, so may this couple perform and keep the vow and covenant made between them, and may they ever remain in perfect love and peace together and live according to your laws through Jesus Christ our Lord. Amen."

[If the parties desire, the man shall at this time hand a ring to the minister, who will return it to him and direct him to place it on the third finger of the woman's left hand. And the man shall say to the woman, repeating after the minister,

"With this ring, I thee wed, and with all my worldly goods, I give you, in the name of the Father, and of the Son, and of the Holy Ghost. Amen."]

Then the minister shall join their right hands together and say, "Seeing that _____ and _____ have consented together in holy wedlock, and have witnessed the same before God and this company, and thereto have pledged their faith to each other, and have declared the same by joining of hands, I pronounce that they are husband and wife in the name of the Father, and of the Son, and of the Holy Ghost. Those whom God has joined together, let no man put asunder. Amen."

And the minister shall add this blessing: "God the Father, the Son, and the Holy Ghost, bless, preserve, and keep you; the Lord mercifully look upon you with His favor and so fill you with all spiritual blessing and grace that you may so live together in this life that in the world to come you may have life everlasting. Amen."

Then the minister shall offer the following prayer: "Oh God of Abraham, God of Isaac, God of Jacob, bless this man and this woman and sow the seeds of eternal life in their hearts that whatsoever they shall profitably learn in your Holy Word, they may indeed fulfill. Look mercifully, Lord, on them from heaven and bless them. As you sent your blessings upon Abraham and Sarah for their great comfort, so grant your blessings upon this man and this woman, that they, obeying your will and always being in safety under your protection, may abide in your love to the end of their lives through Jesus Christ our Lord.

"Almighty God, who at the beginning created our first parents, Adam and Eve, and sanctified and joined them together in marriage, pour the riches of your grace upon these two persons, sanctify and bless them, that they may please you in body and soul, and live together in holy love until the end of their lives. Amen."

Here the minister may use extemporaneous prayer. Then the minister shall repeat the Lord's Prayer: "Our Father who art in heaven, *holy is your name. Your kingdom come. Your will be done on earth, as it is in heaven. Give us this day our daily bread, and forgive us our trespasses, as we forgive them that trespass against us; and lead us not into temptation, but deliver us from evil, for yours is the kingdom, and the power, and the glory, forever. Amen.*"

The Wedding Day

> Hail wedded love! mysterious law, true source
> Of human offspring, sole propriety
> In Paradise: of all things common else.
> Far be it I should write you sin or blame,
> Or think you unbefitting holiest place,
> Perpetual fountain of domestic sweets![1]
>   – John Milton

It is your wedding day! Long anticipated but here at last! Once it seemed as though the long, dragging hours would never reach this happy time, but God has been better than all your fears, and has brought you to the longed-for goal. Hearty congratulations! May the hours of today be as brimful of joy as flowers and music, the good wishes of the old and the mirth of the young, as the blessing of God and man can make them. And when twenty-five or fifty summers have come and gone,

---
[1] John Milton, *Paradise Lost,* 1667.

may this day be celebrated by you and your twin soul as the threshold of a union of ever-increasing blessedness.

The bridegroom will surely be up at the break of day, so he can linger over his prayers, prayers in which thanksgiving and petitions will mingle: thanksgiving that He who said, *It is not good that the man should be alone* (Genesis 2:18), and who made man, male and female, neither complete without the other, has brought to him the woman who shall complete his nature and make his paradise; and petition that he may be able to meet the trust committed to him by the woman's heart, which has abandoned itself to his keeping, foregoing all others who may have counted it an honor to serve her tiniest whim, and that in him the full meaning of her being may be realized and completed.

And won't the bride pause before Him who implanted in her nature that trustful love whose instincts she has followed with prayer? No hand can still her fluttering heart, no voice can reassure, and no presence can deepen the inward bliss like His who at Cana made common water redden into the luscious sanctified wine.

There can be no doubt as to the divine institution and authority of marriage. From the time of man's innocence in Eden, it has had the divine blessing. And Jesus expressly gave the approval of the new covenant to the original command, when He reiterated the ancient words that a man should leave his father and his mother and cleave to his wife and that they would be one flesh. Tender are the ties of home with the mother that bore, the sister that tended, and the father that watched the onset of life and taught the boy to shoot his first arrow, kick his first ball, or take his first dive. All these must yield in strength and tenacity to the call of that masterful love which says of two lives, "You shall no longer be two, but one."

The Hindu holds that man is only a complete being when he becomes a triad – man, woman, child. We dare not go so far, for the light of these Christian centuries shines clearly on noble characters which have been nurtured in loneliness. In many saints it has seemed as though the man and the woman, the strong and the tender, the full-grown and the childlike, have blended into one personality. Above all, the holy and complete character of our Master, Jesus Christ, the one perfect flower that has unfolded from the stem of our race, forbids the idea that we can only be perfected through marriage. Still, it is true for most of us that the way to the fullest life is through marriage and the discipline of the home.

> Jesus Christ forbids the idea that we can only be perfected through marriage.

It is a solemn as well as a happy thought that the union is for life. As the familiar formula puts it, the marriage will continue *till death us do part.* One exception exists, which by its very nature violates the marriage bond; there is no power that can dissolve the sacred union of man and wife in matrimony. On one occasion, during His matchless life, our Lord was assailed with the question, *Is it lawful for a man to put away his wife for every cause?* (Matthew 19:3). One party among the Jews held that divorce was legitimate on the ground of the least dislike the husband might have toward his wife, and this was without doubt in their minds when they asked their question. Our Lord did not hesitate but led them back to the origin of marriage, where God made one woman for one man and commanded man to cleave to her. *What therefore God hath joined together, let not man put asunder. And I say unto you, Whosoever shall put away his wife, except it be for fornication, and shall marry another, committeth adultery: and whoso marrieth her which is put away commits adultery* (Matthew 19:6, 9). From the decision of those lips, there can be no appeal. And for you, their chief meaning and importance lies in the blessed assurance that you two, made for each other, as you have so often said, are deemed from this day, by God and man, as inseparably one.

Good-hearted wishes are sent your way: that the wedding ceremony may pass without a hitch; that the home festivities may combine grave and gaiety, tears and laughter, like April weather but with more sun than showers. It might not be out of place, however, to remind you to send some of the flowers and other decorations to the poor or the orphaned children that they may rejoice with you.

From the door of many homes, old shoes were thrown after the carriage in which the happy pair drove from the bride's home for their honeymoon. This is said to have originated in the Jewish custom referred to in the book of Ruth of transferring authority by taking off and handing over the shoe. If this is so, the idea was that the father transferred to the bridegroom the right of putting his foot on the neck of the bride – an altogether odious and barbarous concept. Our modern fashion of throwing handfuls of rice as a token of the wish that there would never be a lack of necessaries in the new home is preferred. It seems to be reminiscent of the old Aryan homesteads in the Far East where rice is the main foodstuff.

Now the long-expected hour of union has come, but it must be remembered that each must think more of the other than of self. Neither must make self-indulgence or selfish pleasure the rule of thought or action. Each must think of the other more than of self. Each must place the health, the well-being, the comfort, the inclination of the other first. And if a conflict comes as to which shall yield most to the other, then as being the stronger of the two, the husband must consider what is best from the viewpoint of the true welfare of the woman entrusted to him. He must always be the girded partner, the watchful eye, quick to detect the first trace of fatigue or over-wearied nerves. It is for him to exert the strong will of his constraint because she is the weaker of the two.

> Reason and the recognition of the presence of Christ must always influence all the relationships of our lives.

In the sacred ties of marriage, there should be the same reverence, delicacy, and purity that have prevailed in the preceding months or years of courtship. Reason and the recognition of the presence of Christ and His holy angels must always influence all the relationships of our lives. Whether we eat or drink or whatever we do, may we do all to the glory of God, always bearing in mind that nothing which God has created can in itself be common or unclean, unless it is desecrated by the selfish and unholy passion of man.

Shouldn't the reading of the Word of God and prayer cast a halo of blessing on this memorable day? Doesn't the very excess of joy call for united expression to the Giver of all good? Isn't there a need that husband and wife should together commit to Him the keeping of their sacred treasure, that He might guard it from any injury it might suffer from their mistake or sin? And in their prayers, let them not forget the hearts that sorely miss them in the family circles they have left.

The Honeymoon

One heart, one mind, one soul, and one desire,
A kindred fancy, and a sister fire
Of thought and passion; these can Love inspire,
This makes a heaven of earth; for this is Love.[2]

Where you may have chosen to spend your honeymoon does not fall within my right to inquire. This will have been determined before this book came into your hands. Its locality perhaps does not matter much, as long as it gives you time to grow together. Nothing could be worse than an attempt to combine this with a tour of cities and their inevitable visits to art galleries, museums, and other sights. Your only art gallery should be the pillared vista of the woods or the slopes of the swelling hills, which clear lakes reflect. Your sights should be the illumination of the morning

---

2   William and Robert Chambers, "Love Is Not Made Of...," *Chambers's Journal* (19th and 20th centuries).

tint or the evening glow on the snowy mountains afire with sunlight.

It is certain that nature always arrays herself in her most attractive dress for eyes that are lit with love. The sun seems to never have shone before, nor the birds to have sung. Such blue was never in God's heaven and such green never on the earth as that which greets love's young sight. Spring's apron never scattered such flowers, and summer's portraying hand never displayed such colors as those that love detects everywhere in the first glad ecstasy of her joy. It is as though she had anticipated the accent of those mighty lips, which shall one day cry, *Behold, I make all things new* (Revelation 21:5); and at her summons there emerged a world in which there should be no more tears, nor pain, nor death, because the former things had passed away forever. Even the familiar faces and scenes of ordinary life are transfigured as when the light shone on Stephen's face from the opened heavens.

Cherish these glad hours. Let them be the chosen time for the blending of the two hearts, the breaking down of any remaining barriers, and the molding of wills. It will be easier now than ever after to learn how to yield utterly to each other, while preserving individuality and self-respect: individuality, because neither must be content to be an echo or shadow of the other; and self-respect, because love is founded on respect, and we cannot love, though we may pity, those whom we have ceased to respect. Let each always act so that the twin soul may have no reason to be ashamed in the hour of calm reflection and retrospect.

In the heat of love, two natures may be so bonded as to become one, each compensating for the other's variations that they may together keep perfect tune in heat and cold. But let the bonding come naturally and spontaneously. Do not force it. Let each reverence and respect the nature of the other and not break in on the temple shrine with a ruthless foot; but on the other hand, let there be no reserve, no coy or shy restraint, no refusal to share the secret treasures of hope, or anticipation, or ambition, or desire. To shut out one another from any chamber of the soul may sow seeds of alienation and estrangement in days after, that will mar the perfect unity and bliss essential to a really happy union.

> If either one has secrets or plans apart from the other, a barrier is at once formed which will grow into an impassable wall.

This stands to reason, for it is only in complete fellowship in all interests that the two can be one. If either one has secrets, plans, friendships, or places of resort apart from the other – subjects on which one cannot speak, doors into chambers one cannot open, envelopes one cannot tear – a barrier is at once formed, which will grow into an impassable wall. A tiny rift is opened in the lute, which will silence all the music of the life.

The wifely heart yearns to be admitted into the secrets of the one she loves and to open hers to him. But how can this be, unless there is that common understanding between them that makes the exchange of confidences easy, and from which, as a common meeting ground, they may pass on into that complete merging of soul with soul, which is the very crown of love. If this understanding and meeting place are not discovered by the end of the honeymoon, there is every fear that the house will begin to show tears and cracks seriously endangering its stability.

There is nothing better, as we shall see later, than to find some common interest in which both can share, and there is no better time for commencing its pursuit, whether it is the study of poetry or the collection of natural specimens, than during the days of the honeymoon. I have always felt that the surest guarantee of a happy married life is to be found not in the contrariness of opposites, but in the agreement of similar tastes and pursuits. If there is no bond of common interest; if everything that fascinates the one must be explained to the other; if tastes, dispositions, and idiosyncrasies lie far apart, then a deep, unfulfilled desire for sympathy will begin to develop. Before either has realized it, there will be a severance of perfect unity, a slow drift apart, which like the minute crack in the ice floe, widens every moment.

Perhaps the woman can best prevent this by throwing herself into her husband's hobbies. Not that she must merge her identity in his anymore than that perfect music, which answers perfect words, ceases to be music. She will always look at every question from her woman's point of view, and with the quick intuition of her heart, there will be a response, a perfect harmony, an unaffected interest with whatever things are just, lovely, and of good report that may be occupying her husband.

One of the happiest marriages was that of Robert

Browning and Elizabeth Barrett, each of them gifted with the poet's soul more than most. Her Portuguese sonnets are an unequaled confession of woman's love, and there was a world of meaning in his kneeling on the steps of Marylebone Church after her death. He kissed the spot on which she had walked on their wedding day. In each of these noble souls, though they rarely spoke to each other of the specific poems that they were engaged in writing, there dwelt a similarity of disposition, taste, and viewpoint. Of course, where there is such similarity of taste and genius, as in this case, care must be exercised that there is no rivalry, no jealousy, no competition, and no opportunity of comparison. It is a mistake for a woman to purposefully compete so she may speak better or paint better than her husband. Yet, after making all possible deductions, the best advice we can give is that the best security of happiness is in similarity of interest, natural or acquired. The story is told of a girl who detested mathematics until she lost her heart to a mathematics professor, and then she fell in love with mathematics also.

When husband and wife are one in Christ, a new source of mutual affection is opened to them. So far from their prayers being hindered, they are greatly helped. Each watches over the spiritual welfare of the other with tender attentiveness, encouraging further experiences in the divine life, and sharing whatever new discoveries have been made in the unsearchable riches of Christ. Thus, in the deepest and holiest relationship, they that fear the Lord speak often to one another, and the Lord draws near to listen; a book of remembrance is written before Him for those who think upon His name. The more we love each other, the more we learn of the nature of God who is love, and as we know His love, we love each other even more. Thus human and divine love answer each other, and like reflecting mirrors, they act and react on each other endlessly.

It is good to pray, each audibly, and to read the Bible together. To do this from the beginning will be easier than at any subsequent moment. Did our Lord refer to such fellowship when He spoke of being especially with two who met in His name and agreed in the symphony of perfect musical accord? Nothing will more quickly detect any division of feeling or bring together two souls in mutual confession, forgiveness, and agreement. But this most sacred exercise must never be a substitute for solitary personal fellowship with God. However close our relationship is with another, it can never take the place of fellowship with Him. We must continually enter into the most Holy Place, each soul by itself. To each most loving wife or husband, the command must apply: *When thou prayest, enter into thy closet, and when thou hast shut thy door, pray to thy Father which is in secret* (Matthew 6:6).

A radiant, soul-knitting honeymoon to you both!

What the Wife Expects from Her Husband

Let husband know
Their wives have sense like them. They see,
And smell,
And have their palates both for sweet
And sour,
As husbands have.[3]
   – William Shakespeare

I wonder did you ever count
The value of one human fate;
Or sum the infinite amount
Of one heart's treasures, and the weight
Of Life's one venture, and the whole
Concentrate purpose of a soul.[4]
   – Adelaide Anne Procter

---

3   William Shakespeare, *Othello,* Act IV, scene iii, 1603.
4   Adelaide Anne Procter, "For the Future," Sept. 8, 1860.

A woman gives much to a man; indeed, she gives *all*. Before marriage, she may have been the center of a large circle of admirers and lovers who were sworn to do her tiniest bidding; all courtesy, all tenderness, all that love or money could procure were gladly hers. But when she marries, all this ends, and can never be renewed in that form.

How needful, then, that he who now assumes sole charge should fulfill his part that she may not be disappointed or cast glances of regret over the vanished past as having been happier and better in every way.

Brothers, the sisters whom we have asked to share our lives with us are still women with the woman's heart strong within them, counting on the life with us to be better than their former freedom. They hope our love will compensate them fully for all that they have forsaken by our call. By the vows we made when we sought their hand, the pledge we committed at the marriage altar, and the love we bore and bear, let us not give needless pain. There will necessarily be suffering when business calls us into life's battle, when life goes against us, and when through sorrow they bear our children, but let us not add tears and stabs through our carelessness or sin.

They have a right to claim that we should *love and cherish* them. "For better, for worse; for richer, for poorer; in sickness, and in health, to love and to cherish, till death us do part," as we said once. The second word amplifies and enforces the first. Our love may be strong, but silent; it may be true, but lacking in expression; it may be deep, but restrained. We may assure our souls that there is so perfect an understanding between us and our wives that there is no need for the incessant reiteration and assurance. The vows have never been unsaid; the pledges never cancelled, and though there has been no recent confirmation, there has been no withdrawal. Therefore it may be taken for granted that everything remains in force as on the wedding day! Thus we argue, and yet all the while the woman's heart may be craving for some assurance, a tiny word, or look, or smile – something to feed upon as a sweet morsel and turn to as she did with the first letter or gift.

The woman's heart craves tenderness, not simply for love's dues but also for its dues tenderly expressed: the apples of gold in pictures of silver, the jewel in its casket, and all wrapped in soft tissue paper. And so, while one apostle says that the husband is not to be bitter against his wife, and reminds him that she is the weaker vessel and therefore too frail to stand the jar and shock of rough words, another goes further and bids the husband to nourish and cherish his wife as he would his own flesh. *So ought men to love their wives as their own bodies. He that loveth his wife loveth himself. For no man ever yet hated his own flesh; but nourisheth and cherisheth it, even as the Lord the church* (Ephesians 5:28-29).

> While one apostle says that the husband is not to be bitter against his wife, the weaker vessel, another bids the husband to cherish his wife as he would his own flesh.

> If I leave all for you, will you exchange
> And be all to me? Shall I never miss
> Home-talk and blessing and the common kiss
> That comes to each in turn? ...
> Nay, will you fill that place by me which is
> Filled by dead eyes too tender to know change? ...
> Alas, I have grieved so I am hard to love.
> Yet love me—will you? Open thine heart wide,
> And fold within, the wet wings of your dove.[5]
> – Elizabeth Barrett Browning

Let us ask ourselves, are we tender enough? Do we nourish and cherish those whom we have sworn to defend?

Might we not have something to regret if we were suddenly called to stand beside the grave? Perhaps a few flowers now would be better than handfuls then, and a loving word today better than an elaborate epitaph hereafter; never bitterness on the one hand but the cheery smile, the kind word, the loving expression on the other.

The wife expects to always be the husband's queen, that the light of love should never die out of his eyes or the greeting fade from his face when they meet. The true woman is quite content to have one loyal subject; the walls of her home are the sufficient boundaries of her realm.

She expects also that her husband should treat her as a reasonable being with whom he can hold conversation on matters that are filling the public mind, being discussed in newspapers, and deserving careful

---

[5] Elizabeth Barrett Browning, *Sonnets from the Portuguese 35*: "If I leave all for thee, wilt thou exchange," 1850.

consideration on the part of each member of the community. She further expects that her husband will not always give her his most tired moments when he comes back from the exciting meeting or the absorbing pursuit of business. She will surely tend to him in those hours of reaction and be quite ready to sit beside him in silence until the tired nervous system has recovered. But she does expect that he will not always reserve his vivacity for the larger circles of society, and that her life will be cheered by his brightest smiles, his most sparkling wit and pleasantry, and his exuberant spirit. For often it happens that the wife carries a secret pain in her heart because others seem able to touch the chords of her husband's life with a lighter, more delicate touch than she can. We must take care, my brothers, to give sparkling water to those who love us best, not always to that which is flat and hot.

The wife's heart yearns for the husband to take an interest in what she prepares, whether it is some dainty dish which he is fond of, or a dress she has put on in honor of some special occasion, or a delicate touch of womanly grace in their home. "I wonder if he will notice it," she asks herself. If he doesn't, she is a little disappointed. She expects that from his side, he will meet her with little surprises on his return from distant journeys, or now and again when there has been a special windfall of success, or on recurring anniversaries of birth or wedding day, she hopes he will bring home some trifle to show that he does not forget.

Never forget that the joy of married life is very delicately poised; balance is affected this way or that by trifles. If we are attentive to these, the supreme bliss within our reach may be attained.

It may be that when the first week or two of married life is over, you awake to the realization of a great mistake. The girl you had taken to complete your life is not all you had hoped. There is something in her behavior, habits, way of looking at things, or manner toward others that threatens to become a source of perpetual trial. You are the soul of order, she is untidy; you are punctual to the stroke of a moment, she is always late; you are accurate in every detail of your speech, she colors and exaggerates; you are frank and easy, she stands on ceremony and etiquette.

What do you do then? When the first disappointment is over, you may have bent your back beneath your burden with a stoic's strength, and as nature casts out a hard growth to cover the tender skin where the shoe pinches or the burden rubs, you may have settled into a grim and hard indifference. It is your fate, you said. And it is out of this that the lack of tenderness, of which we spoke before, probably sprang. It is not invariably so, because we may be too careless and self-absorbed – but often it is so.

There is a more excellent way. Do not evade the yoke, but take it. Set yourself to remove these spots and wrinkles and present this life to yourself without one of them. Go on showing tenderness, if you have not dropped it. Or, if you have, begin to give yourself to it, though it might at first be from a stern and unbending sense of duty. Deny yourself; make her first; tell her gently of what in her behavior hurts you most. Don't lose your temper when, again and again, she forgets your words; give yourself, as Christ did, to the cross of self-denial. By your suffering and prayer, cleanse her; do not speak to man or woman, but to God. Never abandon your high quest, and never rest until you have lifted her to your ideal; love must conquer.

Begin today, though the marriage wreaths have withered almost to dust. Do not wait to feel as you should. Purpose to do the right thing; behave in the right way; compel yourself to act according to the highest standards. And as you step out and begin to act out love in God's name, His love will fill the channel which your act provides. The emotions and sentiment will follow, and at last the old smile, the old tenderness, and the old kiss will come again.

> Don't lose your temper when, again and again, she forgets your words; give yourself, as Christ did, to the cross of self-denial.

One of the greatest of our modern storytellers narrates the experience of a man who, within a month after marriage, awoke to know that he had made a profound mistake. But he locked the secret in his heart and braced himself to a heroic task. He would never let her know; he would never waken her from her dream. She should think herself his ideal, the queen of his heart, and know no disillusion. And as he strove, he realized that a new love was awakening – not the love of pity but the love of love, which made life blessed. It was a stronger, nobler, purer, more enduring tie than could have sprung from sentiment or whim, and it made him hero and saint. Go and do likewise.

What the Husband Expects from His Wife

A wife, domestic, good, and pure,
Like snail, should keep within her door;
But not, like snail, with silver track,
Place all her wealth upon her back.[6]
   – William Walsham How

Even in the happiest choice, where fav'ring heaven
Has equal love and easy fortune given,
Think not the husband gained that all is done;
The prize of happiness must still be won;
And often the careless find it to their cost
The lover in the husband may be lost:
The graces might alone his heart allure;
They and the virtues meeting must secure.[7]
   – Lord George Lyttelton

---

6   William Walsham How, "Good Wives."
7   Lord George Lyttelton, "Advice to a Lady," 1731.

First and foremost, her husband, according to the unequaled description of the ideal wife given in the closing chapters of the book of Proverbs, must feel that he is able to safely trust her. Everything hinges here. She should not tell his secrets or discuss him with her confidantes; she should be faithful and careful in the administration of his money; she should be absolutely innocent in her relations with all other men, not seeking their admiration or accepting their private adoration. The surest way to forfeit a man's love and heart is to be unfaithful to him. The surest way to keep them is to lock up his words and secrets as in a golden casket, giving the key to no one, but wearing it in the heart. Happy the husband who can safely trust his wife; he will always have a quiet, sheltered haven in which to repair his tempest-driven bark. And happy the woman who knows how to listen, how to draw out, and how to keep her husband's secrets. She will do him good and not evil all the days of her life.

> Happy the husband who can safely trust his wife; he will always have a quiet, sheltered haven in which to repair his tempest-driven bark.

A woman should not use her knowledge of her husband's matters to help him in her own way. I remember a case in which this was done. Knowing her husband's difficulties with a certain individual, without consulting him she sent for this person and tried to adjust matters. This resulted in greatly aggravating the situation, for this man's first thought was that the husband was a coward for not dealing with him directly. He finally lost his temper with the wife for presuming to meddle.

Then, when the husband learned of what had happened, it seemed to shatter his trust, and from that moment until years gone by had healed the wound, he could not resume the old perfect interchange of thought. You may mend a fractured globe of glass, but there will always be the crack.

Fenelon says of the duties of a wife: "Let her love her husband next to her God; let her submit to him with mildness and obey him with cheerfulness; let her deserve his confidence by her discretion, her modesty and reserve."[8] There is no doubt that, in the view of the New Testament writers, the husband is the head of the wife, as Christ should be of every man and must be of His church. And that shunned word *obey* is certainly and unhesitatingly used by the apostle Peter, while *submission* is stressed by the apostle Paul. I am not unaware of the attempts which have been made to minimize the force of these words by the suggestion that they emanated from men's prejudices and were colored by the usages of the time. My belief in the power and teaching of the Holy Spirit forbids my diluting the instructions that He has inspired. And from first to last, all Scripture gives the impression that, except where her duty to God interferes, the woman's nature should yield to the man's.

In that rarest of all mausoleums erected for love of woman, the magnificent Taj at Agra, in which the dome of pure white marble soars high in the clear air

---

[8] Monsr. François de Salignac de la Monthe-Fénelon, Archbishop of Cambray, *Extracts from The Religious Works of Monsr. Francois Salignac de la Mothe Fenelon, Archbishop of Cambray,* Translated by Miss Marshall, Bookseller to Her Majesty (London: J. Hatchard and Son, Piccadilly, 1809), 267.

over the tomblike monument of a tenderly loved wife and queen, I noticed that the slab above her remains was fashioned like a slate. However, the slab above her husband's, who was interred nearby, resembled a pen box, because according to the thought of that age, the woman presents her nature to her husband as a slate, on which he may write what legend he will. This thought is in harmony with the Scriptures we have quoted, and both agree with the ordinary instinct of human society, which almost considers it a breach of nature when the woman, as in Burma, takes the lead and does the business, while man is effeminate and weak.

But in a rightly ordered marriage, these issues never occur. Or at least, relations must have become terribly strained when they do. No loving husband will command his wife, and no true wife will hesitate to count his wish as law whenever it is clearly expressed and consistent with her loyalty to God, the nature He gave her, and the children to whom she has given birth. But none of these considerations could be ignored by a true man.

> They were so one, it never could be said
> Which of them ruled, or which of them obeyed:
> He ruled because she would obey, and she,
> By obeying him, ruled as well as he.
> There ne'er was known between them a dispute
> Save which the other's will should execute.

That a woman should love her husband need hardly be repeated; only let it be noted that such love will find expression. A woman must carefully maintain the little arts and tendernesses of the courting days – not coy, nor artful, not peevish, nor irritable. She needs to not push needlessly her preferences and dislikes, or make much of insignificant and trifling trials; but she needs to be sweet, bright, tender, inviting the caress, and quick to respond to the first movement of love and return it. Perhaps she might not always wait for him to woo her, but go to him with welcomes that speak in sparkling eyes, outstretched arms, and kisses that are as fresh as the breath of the sea.

Whatever may have been the trials and worries of the day, the wife should try to greet the husband with a loving smile. Let her run to welcome him at the door as she once did, and accompany him to the doorstep when he must go forth to meet the world. "The soul's armor is never well set to the heart, unless a woman's hand has braced it – and it is only when she braces it loosely, that the honor of manhood fails."[9]

And why shouldn't she dress herself as tastily and daintily now as she did when on tiptoe she listened for the step of her lover? She must not spend their common money on trifles or extravagant dresses, but she can always dress neatly, tastefully, and prettily. And if she must wear the same dress till its colors are somewhat faded, a woman will always find a way of making it appear different – with a flower, a ribbon, or a piece of lace. But it is good to keep the habit of dressing to

---

9   John Ruskin, *Sesame and Lilies* (New York: John Wiley & Son, 1865).

receive him when he comes home tired and wearied. Not that he cares about the dress, but he cares much for the love that prompted the thought.

And then, how necessary it is to be punctual, to have everything ready, to be on the spot! To miss that first moment is to miss the froth of the new milk, the dew of the young day! How good to have some thoughts ready to keep the fire of conversation from dying to gray ashes. How wise to be able to look on the bright side of what has depressed and tested the agitated worker and to avoid adding to his worries by enumerating the vexations of the day! He will be willing to hear them presently, when the worries of the day have receded. Then he should hear them, or there is the danger of an estrangement creeping in. How marvelously a wise and prudent woman can extract the sting from the wound or the poison from the hurt, and how often a wife's wise counsel has averted a mistake and suggested a prudent and sound policy, thus fulfilling the ancient couplet of the sage:

> *She openeth her mouth with wisdom;*
> *And in her tongue is the law of kindness.*
> – Proverbs 31:26

There are dark, sad days in all our lives, but a wife's love shines then as the lighthouse beside the fort. Bearing, believing, hoping, and enduring all things, her love, like God's, never fails. Her idol may have been shattered. She may have awakened to find her husband further than she expected. She might sit among the ruins of her hopes, not daring to tell another her sad secret. But she will unburden her sorrow to God and pray, and be patient, and wait; she will continue to do her duty in the home and for her husband, as she did when all the landscape was bright. She will do so until her task is done, and either her love will conquer, or God will take her to His bosom where broken hearts are forever comforted and healed.

Many a husband expects from his wife more than he has any right to expect – that she should always yield to him; that she should always be sweet, cheerful, patient, and forbearing; that she should be willing to mind the home while he goes out to his politics, his religious meetings, and his pleasures. Take care, husbands, lest you bend the bow to breaking and stretch the worn string till it snaps. Remember, there must be a reciprocity in the give-and-take of married life, and if you ask for so much, be sure to accept it with thanks, frank acknowledgment, and the renewed expressions of endearment which cheer lonely hours and make a light like heaven's smile hover over your vacant seat the many hours you are gone from home.

Difficult Marriages

I do not love you less for what is done,
And cannot be undone. Your very weakness
Hath brought you nearer to me, and henceforth
My love will have a sense of pity in it,
Making it less a worship than before.
   – Longfellow

They said that Love would die when Hope was gone,
And Love mourned long, and sorrowed after Hope;
At last she sought out Memory, and they trod
The same old paths where Love had walked with Hope,
And Memory fed the soul of Love with tears.
   – Tennyson

Nay, sometimes seems it I could even bear
To lay down humbly this love-crown I wear,
Steal from my palace, helpless, hopeless, poor,
And see another queen it at the door,—
If only that the king had done no wrong,
If this my palace, where I dwelt so long,
Were not defiled by falsehood entering in.[10]
   – Dinah Maria Mulock Craik

---

10 Dinah Maria Mulock Craik, "Living: After A Death" from *Poems: By the Author of "John Halifax, Gentleman"* (Boston: Ticknor & Fields, 1866), 32.

I trust this is a very unlikely supposition. May it never be realized in your life, my friend! Yet, suppose he should cease to love, or she. What then? Suppose he who pledged his faithfulness at the marriage altar should betray it and withdraw what he promised so faithfully. What should the wife do then? He doesn't take the same interest in her or in their common life that he once did; he hardly notices the pretty dress or the attractive way of fixing her hair. He sits at the table without speaking a word or answers her remarks with monosyllables; he quickly leaves the table under the excuse of pressing work.

Perhaps he is ill, and the wifely heart is full of anxiety. Perhaps business is unusually absorbing and vexatious, and she must not worry him. But her heart turns faint with nameless dread. Surely, if either of these suppositions were correct, he would return to his old glad, bright self! But days grow into weeks and weeks into months, and the clouds brood more heavily than ever, where once blue skies and brilliant sunshine promised to be perpetual. And then, suddenly, the thought flashes upon her that she is no longer what she was, and perhaps his heart has drifted elsewhere as a man may turn the gleam of a lantern, now here, now there! What shall she do? It is useless to scold. That will do no good, and it may alienate him further. To escape her pelting words, he will hide himself under the cloak of some such excuse as this: "Oh, if only I were free from her! Doesn't this outburst prove how little she understands me or can sympathize with my temperament and character?"

It is unwise to tell others rather than God. In matters of this kind, it is utterly impossible to expect man or woman to keep your secret. The walls have ears. Love itself will let your secret slip, as quicksilver from the most tenacious grasp. No, you must not involve him or yourself in scandal, which at first will be whispered in the closet but eventually proclaimed upon the housetops. Instead, pour out your heart before God and let the walls of your chamber witness your strong cries and tears; let the whispered prayers of Hannah be your model, and though men like Eli misjudge you, you will certainly find that God will show Himself strong on your behalf. It may be that weary years will pass before the answer is given, but you have the petition you desired of Him, and the woman of a sorrowful spirit shall come again to the scene of her supplications and bring her answer, bursting out in songs of triumphant joy.

> It is unwise to tell others rather than God.

It is a mistake to relax your wifely thoughtfulness. When this sorrow comes upon a woman, it paralyzes her. She is suddenly deprived of the motivation that made her life as easy as the quiver of a hummingbird over a flower. In her dress, her housekeeping, her little personal adornments, there had always been one reward – that he would be pleased. But now that nothing seems to give him interest, why should she care? There is a tendency then to neglect her appearance, the table, the home, and let all fall into disorder. In many cases, there has been a further abandonment to alcohol and perhaps suicide. But such a relaxation of the strength and tenacity of a life's purpose is profoundly mistaken, for in his secret soul, conscious of wrongdoing, he is in search of some plea of self-justification. He is only too relieved to discover it in this alteration of his wife's behavior, her neglect of his comfort, and the disarray which has occurred in his home.

Least of all, must she permit any flirting with others. This sometimes has been the mistaken direction of disappointed, heart-weary wives. They have resolved to stimulate and recall the flagging affections of their husbands by appearing to favor other men – not that they have really cared for them, but that they were set on trying any strategy to regain their lost love. It is a hazardous experiment. Not only does it seem to afford the faithless husband a fresh justification for his wrongdoing, but the wife could also be drawn into problematic relations with someone whom she secretly despises but uses in her desperation as a pretext.

It seems as though there is no resource but prayer, no line of conduct but patient continuance in well-doing, and no deliverance but His appearance who, when the storm was highest, came across the waves, bringing cheer and salvation. At His rebuke, the tempest will become calm; and through His grace, working in illness, or disappointment, or disaster, the cause of alienation will disappear, while the heart will recognize and leap to embrace its twin heart, as in the former time.

But suppose that *she* has ceased to love, my brother, and there is no response to your fond approaches. What then? This will not justify you in going elsewhere. You have no alternative but to wait for the Lord's pleasure and in the meantime show her all kindly and thoughtful attention. A working man's life was once brought to my attention, which illustrates what I mean. After his conversion, his wife developed a violent dislike for him and gave him no peace. However, he did not retort except with additional kindness and rose early enough to be able to do some of the heaviest chores in their cottage before going to his own laborious work. During the first week, he lit the kitchen fire and put the kettle to boil. But she never said a word. In the following week, he added to this the drawing of the water from the well. But she still appeared to take no notice.

He continued with the same behavior for months, except he was always adding new items. But one night his wife threw herself beside him and asked how he could continue when she had treated him with such unfeeling emotion, and he told her that it was not he but Christ in him that had stood victorious through the fiery test. Before they retired to rest, she had become as a little child in the kingdom of God. We must not be weak and timid, lacking in loving expressions and appeals to the better sense; but for the most part, the consistent life, the appeal of unselfish deeds, and our unswerving loyalty to the highest ideals of Christian manhood will, by God's blessing, win the day.

It is most important that a man never relinquish the high aim and purpose of his career because he is deprived of that wifely cooperation on which he once counted. The greatest victories are those that are snatched from imminent defeat or are won apart from the usual conditions of success. Clive's victories at Plassey and Arcot, for instance, were more remarkable because they were gained in the face of overwhelming numbers and when his soldiers were in desperate need of rest, ammunition, and food.

God allows these awful sorrows to come into our lives to test us and to afford an opportunity for the manifestation and growth of the noblest and most unselfish qualities of the soul. These are the battlefields where the rarest laurels are won. These are the arenas where, in feats of endurance and patience, souls attain the rank of *the first three mighties* (1 Chronicles 11) in the court of the Son of God. And when the lesson has been learned, God's "Jacobs" go forth as "Israels," wounded, maimed, limping until they die, but ennobled, royal, and able to scatter blessings, as when Pharaoh bent beneath the trembling hand of the aged patriarch. Out of such experiences, men and women are able to help others, to communicate comfort, to lighten the heavy burdens, and to give comfort to fainting hearts. And when beneath their touch and voice despairing ones develop a new hope, seize again the shield and sword, and plunge into the fight for purity, truth, and self-denial, they see the fruit of their tears, and their prayers are rewarded.

One often thinks of the myriads particularly in Eastern lands who have never known love. And comparing the cases considered in this chapter with theirs, who does not feel that it is better to suffer a lasting regret or an inevitable pain than to not have had the ideal, to not have realized the capacity for love's best gift? No, man or woman, always be glad that you have dreamed love's fairest dreams, even though, like the Naiad's footsteps on the sands, they have left no trace except in memory. Cherish those high and holy imaginings; someday, somewhere, they shall be realized in fact, and God shall give you your heart's desires. In the meantime, guard against cynicism, pessimism, and despair.

The Home

Home's not merely four square walls,
Though with pictures hung and gilded;
Home is where Affection calls—
Filled with shrines the Hearth hath builded! . . .

Home's not merely roof and room,
It needs something to endear it;
Home is where the heart can bloom,
Where there's some kind heart to cheer it![11]
    – Charles Swain

Take care that neither of you speak of the home as *my* home or even *my* house; it must be *our* home, *our* house. And each of you must put honest work into your homelife if it is to realize the ideal.

"If a man and a woman," so says a modern writer,

---

11 Charles Swain, "Home Is Where There Is One to Love Us," *Poems* (Boston: Whittemore, Niles, and Hall, 1857) 204.

"are to live together well, they must take the plant of love to the sunniest and securest place in their habitation. They must water it with tears of repentance or tears of joy; they must jealously remove the destroying insects and pluck off the dead leaves that the living may take their place. And if they think they have any business in this life more pressing than the care and culture of this plant, they are undeserving of one another, and time's revenges will be swift and stern."

One of the first necessities in the homelife is politeness. Why should a man cease to treat his wife as a lady because she is always at his side? Is she not as sensitive to notice an offense and as quick to appreciate a tiny attention as she ever was? Are the trifling courtesies of life robbed of their fragrance because they are given by her husband? If she drops her handkerchief, he must still pick it up, but she must not drop it simply to test him. If she rises to leave the dining room, he must still open the door. If he does not catch what she says, he must still say, "I beg your pardon." He must still save her needless exertion. Let him always act as a knight in the order of Christian gentleness, of Christ's highbred nobility. *Noblesse oblige toujours* (Nobility always obliges). And she must always be the trueborn gentlewoman because she is one of the King's daughters.

> Let the husband always act as a knight in the order of Christian gentleness.

There must also be the willingness to ask pardon and to forgive. Sometimes it has happened that one has been nervously agitated and the other unduly sensitive;

a word has flashed like a sword from its sheath, causing an injury for many an hour afterward, hurting the one who inflicted it even more than the one who suffered. How much better it would be if the unkindness were instantly followed by the frank confession and restoration, like God's, to the old, blessed place of sunlight. This would be far better than to leave the matter to right itself or to act as though it had never happened, as each one surely knows that it has left a scar. It is not enough to bring a present from the city to pacify the sin. Let the poison be pressed out of the wound so it can be properly healed. Let there be the frank confession, by which the two stand together hereafter in a common fight against a common foe.

The home should be founded on Christ. There should be family prayer, either morning or evening, or both. Nothing will so sweeten and purify the homelife as this. The monks who built the cathedrals of the world held that wherever the worship of God is set up, obscene demons hasten to leave the spot. Therefore, they carved the gargoyles at right angles to their buildings, and supposedly, the evil spirits, pledged to mar the blessed-home happiness, flee from where the family gathers for prayer day by day.

But more than this, the spirit of Christ should rule the conversation at the meals, the literature strewn on the side tables, and the expenditure on the household maintenance. Even where it is not constantly mentioned, it should control and mold, for the working of God's providence is evident in no book of the Bible more than in the book of Esther, though His name is never mentioned there from the beginning to the end.

Dr. Horton reminded us that when John Eliot was an usher in Thomas Hooker's school at Little Baddow, he did not tell us that Hooker talked to him, but said, "Here the Lord said to my dead soul – live! And through the grace of Christ, I do live, and I shall live forever. When I came to this blessed family, I then saw, and never before, the power of godliness in its lively vigor and effectiveness." Would that all our homes were filled with the same heavenly and divine spirit, which would attract men as the scent of flowers does the bees. But hearts, like alabaster boxes, must be dedicated to the service of Jesus and broken over His feet before the house can be filled with the odor of the ointment.

We must exercise a rigid self-regimen if the atmosphere of our homes is to be sweet and healthy. Walter Scott always concealed his fits of depression from his friends because, he said, it was bad enough for *him* to bear them without inflicting them on others. And Emerson has said, "One topic is peremptorily forbidden to all rational mortals: namely, their distempers. If you have not slept, or if you have slept, or if you have the headache, or leprosy, or thunderstroke, I beseech you by all the angels to hold your peace, and not pollute the morning. Come into the azure and love the day." It is true, however, that they who hide their own passing phases of gloom must not be careless of the expression of pain or sorrow on the faces of others, but be keen to notice and quick to sympathize. It may be that a little loving tenderness will dissipate the clouds.

The husband should trust the wife with the household expenditures. Let them decide together what style they will adopt and what weekly or monthly sum they can spend; only let it be within their means. Then it is for him to give her the money regularly and for her to lay it out as carefully and judiciously as she knows how. She will do better if she is trusted than if he is always overhauling her methods and inspecting her accounts. Of course, there should be accounts, and once a month they should go through them together. Certainly, she should have enough for dress, for little extras of taste, and for general house expenses. But there must be no debt, and there should be a little saved and put sacredly away for a time of illness, the holidays, or the arrival of the little baby. And she should be told how much he is making, and what the outlook is. If there is more, she will be glad; if less, she will brace herself to economize. All the payments should be in ready cash, no overdue bills, no debts, no long-running accounts. And the money should be in hand before the dress is ordered or the new furniture procured for the house.

> The wife will do better if she is trusted than if he is always overhauling her methods of spending and inspecting her accounts.

These are general principles that must be applied by each couple for themselves, but on the whole, they are sound principles for all, and it is from a lack of these that so many marriages have been wrecked before they have adventured long on life's stormy seas.

William Cobbett tells us that when he saw his future wife, flushed and docile, at the washtub, he said, "That's the wife for me." He began life with as little money as anyone, but he saw no reason why he should not marry; he got his fortune in his wife's serviceableness. Young men will do well to see if, beneath the girl's accomplishments and degrees, she can, at a push, cook a mutton chop and know how long to boil a potato. Of course, a good husband hopes his wife may always be saved from work to which she was not accustomed when he brought her from her father's home, but if she does no household work herself, she should know how it should be done. And I earnestly advise all young women who are about to marry, and young wives who are not quite sure of themselves, to determine to learn how to order a home, cook a dinner, make a dress, and turn faded curtains or carpets. Nothing demeans a true woman but ignorance of her part in making some bare and barren spot cozy and comfortable for him and for her.

Into our homelife, Jesus comes as He did to Cana and Bethany. As at Cana, His presence turns the water into wine, the secular to sacred, the commonplace to consecrated, and the relationship of time to the chalice of the eternal and divine. As at Bethany, He sits at the festive board or on the porch at the close of day, accepting the service of Martha and educating her faith, instructing the heart of Mary into the mysteries of death and resurrection, and preparing her for a supreme act – raising Lazarus from death to life and binding all in one.

Not once beat, "Praise be Thine!
I see the whole design.
I, who saw power, see now love perfect, too!
Perfect I call Your plan!
Thanks that I was a man!
Maker, remake, complete – I trust what You shall do."[12]

– Robert Browning

---

[12] Robert Browning, "Rabbi Ben Ezra," *Dramatis Personae,* 1864.

The Dowry of Children

They are idols of hearts and of households,
They are angels of God in disguise.
   – C. M. Dickenson

Ah! what would the world be to us,
If the children were no more?
We should dread the desert behind us
Worse than the dark before.
   – Longfellow

A little child is a strong uniting bond between husband and wife. Where there had been signs of alienation, those two tiny hands bring hearts and lives together again, and the two streams unite, blended in mutual and common affection. And where there had been true love, that love is woven tighter than before, as the parents bend together over the little life in which their two natures are expressed, no longer two but one.

"The state of marriage," says Bishop Taylor, "fills up the numbers of the elect, is the mother of the world, preserves kingdoms, and fills cities, churches, and heaven itself." This is an aspect of married life that we would be foolish to ignore. What God has cleansed and sanctified, we have no right to call common or unclean. Indeed, there is probably nothing in our human life in which a man approaches so nearly to the great Life-giver as in the passing on of his own life to another. It is a function in our human life that should never be thought of without reverence, or contemplated apart from prayer. And the urgency for this becomes more apparent when we remember that the passion, temper, and disposition of either parent may be so transmitted to the child as to affect its entire afterlife.

> What God has cleansed and sanctified, we have no right to call common or unclean.

If this book were not written for general circulation, I would say more, but I hope that the words already written may be deeply pondered. History, physiology, and experience go to show how inevitably parents impress themselves upon their offspring. If the father wishes the child to be pure-hearted, self-disciplined, strong in character, and godly in aspirations, he must be all that himself. If the mother desires the life, which is so marvelously associated with her own, to attain her ideal, she must realize it herself. What she thinks, the child will think; what she loves, the child will love; what she allows to dominate herself will rule its coming years. For the sake of the child, let her solemnly renounce passion, refuse strong drink, steep her mind in high and holy thoughts, surround herself with sweet sights and sounds, and hold much communion with God.

In the view of God's Word, a small family is a calamity. It was the Creator's original command that man should be fruitful and multiply, and the psalmist says that the father of many sons is like a warrior whose quiver is full of arrows. This view is confirmed by history and experience. The decreasing population of France is becoming a disastrous factor in her history, and is arousing the gravest alarm among her statesmen – so much so, that they are making generous gifts and the promise of free education to the children of large families. They know well enough that a nation with a decreasing population can never become a mighty, colonizing force, but will sink to a lower, inferior rank in the governing of the world. It is to the large families of their peoples that the Anglo-Saxon nations owe their marvelous expansive force, and the world is becoming colonized and dominated by their children.

Doesn't universal experience confirm the verdict of history? What child is so pitiful as an only child, who has been the idol of two people, the spoiled object of their exclusive attention, always associated with their pursuits, and missing the wholesome contact of other children, whether as playmates or fellow students or comrades in adventure? Brothers and sisters refine each other like the pebbles of the sea beach as they roll and tumble with the tides, chipping off corners and rounding the roughest edges into symmetrical shape.

Children of large families usually fare better than an only child. To use the north-country phrase, "They drag each other up." There is a frank *bonhomie,* a chivalrous interest in each other's welfare and a willingness to help each other forward, which are of priceless value in the making of young lives. How good it is for a daughter to have become accustomed to the nursing and care of little brothers and sisters. What an infinite deprivation it is for a girl to never have had a brother, or a brother a sister. Unless the direst considerations of health intervene, no married couple should evade the responsibilities of family life.

Where God sends mouths, He sends the bread to feed them. Those who obey the laws of the Creator may count on Him to provide for them in the results of their obedience to natural law. Sometimes daily bread will be all that He will give, but that is no matter for regret. Rather, it may be counted a crowning mercy if the luxuries which pamper appetite and spoil digestion are withheld. The healthiest families in the world are those that have been reared on little more than oatmeal porridge or good wheat bread.

The nurture of the young child is mostly with the mother. And how sacred the charge! How much she needs of that wisdom that God gives liberally to those who ask! But how certainly may she count on receiving it from Him whose Word said, *Take this child . . . and nurse it for me* (Exodus 2:9). Mothers, let me be dogmatic.

Never say anything to a child that is not perfectly true. Never promise anything that you are not able and prepared to perform. Never lay down conditions for something that you are not prepared to require. Never threaten a child that you will punish him and then omit the infliction. Never tell a child to do a thing and excuse or ignore his disobedience. Never threaten that you will tell his father, as though you could not assert your own authority, for that makes the thought of him a dread rather than a joy. Never pass over a lie, however trivial, or an act of disobedience, however trifling. The tiny fault of today will become a worse one tomorrow. Never tell a child that if he does such and such an act, God or you will cease to love him; you know perfectly well that love is not turned aside by sin. Woe to us if it were!

So much for the negative. As for the positive, your heart will find the clue. Only be consistent; don't be all smiles today and full of touchiness and fretfulness tomorrow. Let your child always find you at home and at leisure. Put away your work and reading when the child seeks you. Be sure to hear morning and evening prayers. Take care not to always delegate your children to the nurse or dispatch them to the nursery, but undertake their training with your own motherly patience and affection. It is better to deny yourself to your friends and to society than to your little ones who bask in your smile as warm sunshine but languish in your absence as in the winter's cold. I am prepared to think that it will better serve a woman's true happiness if she will

> Never threaten that you will tell his father, as though you could not assert your own authority, for that makes the thought of him a dread rather than a joy.

give herself to secure the lasting love of her children, than if she were to shine as the central star in the most brilliant constellation that ever sparkled in society.

The father also has an important part to fulfill. It is not his duty to be always at home, but when he is, it should be a festive time. However much he is engaged, he should give at least one evening a week, and always Sunday, to his wife and children. He doesn't need to always insist on the stronger elements in education, but almost unconsciously he will exercise them. He will mold and guide by what he is, and as the children grow older, he will become their companion and associate to an increasing extent; to be with Father, to be like him, and to do as he does will become the unwritten code of the home. Ah, Father, remember what the lad said when his father and he were climbing the mountainside: "Take the safe path, Father; remember that I am coming." In your habits and self-indulgences, the children will copy you.

> The father will mold and guide by what he is.

What lessons the children teach us! An exquisite poem of Patmore's describes bending over the sleeping form of his child who was sent to his bed, unkissed, because for the seventh time he had disobeyed. He tells how he found the slumbering lashes still wet with tears and added his own; he then turned to God with a plea that He would in like manner bend over him, forgiving folly and sin. Our Lord taught us to reason in this way when He said, *If ye then, being evil, know . . . how much more shall your heavenly Father give?* (Luke 11:13). Our children's simple trust in our patience and strength, their artless love, their retreat to our side in fear and pain, and our own quick response are mirrors in which we see reflections of things which *eye hath not seen, nor ear heard* (1 Corinthians 2:9), but which enter into the heart of man to understand God and His dealings with us.

Common Interests

From this hour the summer rose
Sweeter breathes to charm us;
From this hour the winter snows
Lighter fall to harm us;
Fair or foul, on land or sea,
Come the wind or weather,
Best or worst, whatever they be,
We shall share together.
 – Winthrop Mackworth Praed

Two souls in sweet accord,
Each for each caring and each self unheard,
Bringing life's discords into perfect tune;
True to true feeling, and to nature living,
Plighting no faith, nor needing proof nor proving.
Taking for granted, never asking, giving,
Not doubting, and not fearing "how" or "where"?
Not caring if less bright or young or fair;
Sure to be ever loved, and sure of loving.
 – H. C. Von Ranke

It is of prime importance that husband and wife intertwine their interests. Every additional thing they do together is another bond of union, as long as they do not seek to rival or excel each other, and each helps the other to realize the common aim.

The beginning of this mutual interest in the same things should date from the days of the courtship. The welding of the two metals will be easier in those days than ever after, and what is begun then will continue throughout coming days. Let us review some of the many things in which man and wife may share.

There is, first, their spiritual life. They can read the Bible and pray together, and can go to services and religious meetings and engage in some common Christian work together. How good it is when they become interested in the same poor people, or Sunday school students, or philanthropic organization. They can plan, scheme, and cooperate for the advancement of what lies so near their hearts. Then there is the weekly, monthly, or yearly setting aside of a proportion of the income for the cause of God and the consideration of the best means of applying it.

Next, we may consider the common interest in the home. We might assume that in some cases it will have been furnished by their joint earnings; in others, the husband will have provided the more substantial furniture, while the wife will have procured and perhaps hemmed and marked much of the linen. But however this may be, the arrangement will have been largely a joint affair; the ordering of the plan, the additions that may be made to its ornaments and comforts, and the regulation of the servants will all be matters of mutual interest. Though it should always be remembered that it is the wife's function to engage and superintend the servants, yet she will not fail to enlist her husband's interested advice and suggestions.

Surely, they should also have common pastimes. There is probably one afternoon in the week when in the summer they can mount their bicycles and take a ride into the country; in winter they might go out together for a walk, a skate, or a visit to a picture gallery or a place of recreation. In the course of the year, there will be the holiday trip to the seaside or a mountain, and even if he needs stronger and more vigorous exercise than she has strength for, it will somehow be arranged that they have several days together. It is very beneficial when they can play at some common game. It may seem a trivial remark to make, but it is worthwhile when the man can be induced to relax from the strain of business to play with his wife at chess or backgammon, or whatever else they choose.

To read the same books is also a wholesome bond of union. Lending libraries are within the reach of most of us, and it is very desirable to avail ourselves of the chance to keep in touch with the best new books. When husband and wife are together in the winter evenings, how much good after the meal is done to sit within the enclosed room and take turns reading biographies, poetry, storybooks, or sermons. Here is food for thought and fuel for conversation. And often they may break off from what they read to compare their thoughts, to criticize or admire, or to seek the dictionary or atlas for the explanation of some fresh word or the fixing of a new place on the map. Often the daily press will yield the leading article, the biographical notice, or the report of the great debate as material for the evening study.

A common interest in the same people and friends is all-important. And here the wife needs special wisdom and tact. Of course, there are the friends of either with whom each held happy fellowship in the past. These will be among the first to be welcomed to the new home, and from amongst them, many of the life-friends will probably be gathered. No friends are like those whom one has known and loved first. In those early gatherings, let there be nothing extravagant, nothing of pompousness and display. Be anxious to show how natural and simple true hospitality is, and that your perception of social life consists not in the richness of the cuisine and drinks, but in the wealth of the greeting, the warmth of the heart fellowship, and the brightness and enjoyment of music, pictures, games, and social connection.

In time, other people will call on the wife and introduce her to their friends. The husband will speak from time to time of those whom he has met in business or in committees. These will perhaps be added to the little circle. But care should be exercised to exclude from it the extravagant, the mere creatures of fashion, the irreligious, or those who favor Sunday irreverence. There must be no attempt to strive for the recognition of higher circles by the extravagance of the spendthrift, or the overdone flattery of the brownnoser. All relations with friend and neighbor should be simple, true, straightforward, and sincere.

It will perhaps happen that the wife's quick eye may notice that her husband is attracted to certain unmarried girls who are quite innocent and simplehearted. At first, she may feel a twinge of jealousy like a knife wound in her heart. She will be wise to say nothing and certainly not to find fault with or criticize them. It will obviously be quite as well if she can direct such a course as to not include them in their circle. But if this is impossible, it will be better for her to enter into their friendship with him and to see to it that his friends are her friends too.

Would that these words could be written where every wife might read them. Don't set yourself against your husband's friends. You might not be equally drawn to them and might wish that they had never come into contact, but if he is steadfastly devoted to them, be willing to be pleasant and agreeable. Invite them to your home and act toward them in the power of a God-centered will, showing them all kindness and trusting in your heavenly Father to avert all harm. This is a better policy a thousand times over than to expose him to the temptation of making private arrangements to meet them.

What is addressed to the wife applies, of course, equally to the husband. He must be pleasant to his wife's friends – to her mother and sisters especially.

There need be no friction, no collision between the two homes. But it goes without saying, that where love exists in its warmest, holiest, deepest moods, there will be no difficulty in these matters, because each will read the other's thoughts and detect instantly the shadow cast there by the presence of any against whom there is an incomprehensible but inevitable animosity. This will be sufficient to render it impossible for either to take pleasure in a companionship that might otherwise have been agreeable. One might say here to one's brothers that women are for the most part correct in their intuitions about character, and we would probably be wise if we avoid those about whom our wives have a strong and fixed misgiving.

It is beneficial when a man has a hobby, some special interest, some subject with which he has an extensive and accurate acquaintance. It will give a new adventure to their joint excursions and holidays. Suppose it is botany or zoology; what an arranging of specimens there will be! Suppose it is photography; perhaps *she* will be trusted to develop the negatives. Perhaps it is the violin, and *she* must play the piano accompaniment. Perhaps it is gardening, and *she* will have her share in raking and watering. In boating, *she* can steer; in sailing, *she* may be a whole boat's crew in one. And thus, they grow together as the years pass, and life becomes ever richer. The two streams blend more absolutely than ever, and with increasing volume and deepening channel, they flow toward the bosom of the eternal ocean.

And even if they are called to be severed for weeks or months from each other, they will keep in step, and their hearts will chime across the separating distance. Neither distance nor length of days can sever hearts that meet in God and have found each other. But the hearts that love can fire one another with hidden secret sparks from the opposite ends of the earth – perhaps from heaven. That is why I love so deeply those latter pages in the life of Laurence Oliphant. If you have not read them, read them.

The Retirement Years

John Anderson, my Jo, John,
We clamb the hill thegither.
And mony a canty day, John,
We've had wi' one anither;
Naw we maun totter down, John,
But hand in hand we'll go,
And sleep thegither at the foot,
John Anderson, my Jo.
　– Robert Burns

Hand in hand when our life was May,
Hand in hand when our hair is grey,
Shadow and sun for everyone
As the years roll on.
Hand in hand till the long night tide
Gently covers us, side by side.
Ah, lad – though we know not when –
Love will be with us ever then!
Always the same, Darby, my own,
Always the same to your old wife Joan.
　– F. E. Weatherly

Our faces at fifty, sixty, and seventy tell many tales. They are written over with legends which are hieroglyphics to most, but to which love holds the key. Those gray hairs came in that long absence from each other when the heart was sometimes sick with fear. Those lines around the mouth and eye were the result of that long anxiety over the boy who seemed about to take the wrong turn. Those crow's feet and wrinkles were left by the awful anxiety of that business crisis. Withered, scarred, bent, and old, the watchcase is not in quite the same condition on the golden wedding day as it was on that day fifty years before, which it commemorates. But the love is unchanged. And though winter has cast her frost with lavish hand on the bent head, there is summer – perpetual summer – in the heart.

> Yes, 'tis summer in the heart;
> Snows may fall and teardrops start,
> But the soul that loves, forever
> Keeps summer in the heart.

To the elderly couple, as they sit together on the ridge of the hill of life in the summer twilight, what a glimpse there is backward into the vale through which they have traveled together for so many years! They can now trace the way by which they have been led, and confess that goodness and mercy have followed them all their days. They see where they made mistakes, but these have been forgiven, and the consequences have been neutralized by the magic of the divine grace. They discern the graves over which they bent together, the

Ebenezer stones they reared, the dark, dense woods they traversed, and the sunlit elevations on which they stood hand in hand amid the gleams of prosperity and success. All these live again in their memories which, though difficult to recall the impressions of yesterday, are retentive enough for those of the distant past. Live, young people, with the prospect of that review ahead of you, so when it comes, it may bring you sunny and blessed memories!

Dr. Chalmers used to say that every man should have a Sabbatical decade at the close of his life when, after sixty years of earnest endeavor, he should have ten years for review and rest and preparation for the eternal home. It is to be desired for us all and should be the goal of each of us. It is beneficial when life's toils have brought sufficient remuneration to secure a sufficiency for our last years and for the dear partner of our life. For what can infuse the evening hours of a man's life with more anguish than the knowledge that in the darkening night of his wife's bereavement, there would be the additional pain of threadbare destitution and helpless dependence upon others.

To the elderly, grandchildren are a source of perpetual enjoyment. It is somehow easy for them to become children again with their children's children, and often a comical comradeship springs up between the esteemed grandparent and the grandchild. On the part of the one, there is willingness to listen, ability to spend an unlimited number of hours, and aptness at being greatly interested in the trifles, which weigh so heavily in a child's life. How beautiful are those photographs of Mr. Gladstone and Miss Dorothy Drew, in which the veteran's furrowed face sets off the sweet, cheerful features of his granddaughter!

In response, grandchildren have a patronizing air with the elderly, which is very charming. They lead them off to see their treasures – the dear little kitties, the little ducklings swimming after their mother on the pond, the squirrel that will take his nuts from their hand, or the beautiful big caterpillar that they caught crawling over the gravel path. They admit grandparents into their confidences and hopes, not without some knowledge of their aptitude for spoiling them. They jabber unceasingly of matters which they suppose are as new to the grandparents as to themselves. The little ones indeed seem to think that they have received a charge to be especially mindful of the elderly, and to this they loyally devote themselves.

And so, the elderly couple are still sweethearts. Their love is ripe and mellow. The river may not froth and foam as it did in early days, but it is quieter because it is deeper, fuller, and more weighted with its responsibilities. April with its clouds and sunshine, May with its blooms of promise, June with its maturing beauty, July with its long and unshadowed days, August with its golden colors, and September with its harvests of corn and fruit have yielded to October with its second summer. But there is a slight chill in the air which warns of the fall of the leaf. Yet the love that has lighted their pathway still smiles on them. Were life to start over again, each would choose the other for another spell of fifty years. And the desire is deep in each heart that in death they may not be long divided; no, each thinks that it would be impossible to survive the other and live long alone. But each hopes to close the eyes of the other in the last sleep so that the plight of loneliness and grief may not come upon that other soul which is dearer than self. On such love, faithful and true until death, the angels, on their way home to God, turn aside to look.

Surely for such there must be reunion and companionship in the world where love is supreme. That there will be recognition in that world is not doubtful, thank God. Were there no other proof, it would be sufficient to point out the resurrection of our Lord, in which He was identified by those who had known Him in the days of His flesh. The most incredulous of them recognized Him and cried, *My Lord and my God.* And He addressed Mary in the familiar tone she knew so well, teaching that the intonations of the voice in the spiritual body will not be altogether strange. But there will be more than recognition; there will be love. In his exquisite psalm of love, the apostle anticipates the time when prophecy, tongues, and knowledge shall pass away, while faith, hope, and love shall abide, and the greatest of these is love. In heaven, as Jesus said, they neither marry nor are given in marriage, but those who have loved with an utter devotion and oneness will be permitted the added pleasure of enjoying heaven together. Lovely and pleasant in their lives – surely in death and eternity they will not be divided.

The Bible so often speaks of sitting with Abraham, Isaac, and Jacob in the kingdom of God, placing together grandfather, father, and grandson, that we may cherish the hope that family life will not be entirely obliterated amid "those solemn troops and sweet societies." And when it is promised to Daniel to stand in his lot at the end of the days, it may be that this is referred to. What an assembly that will be, when the successive generations stand together, when the heads and founders of godly families shall meet with their latest descendants, according to the promise: *My spirit that is upon thee, . . . shall not depart out of . . . the mouth of thy seed, nor out of the mouth of thy seed's seed, saith the Lord, from henceforth and for ever* (Isaiah 59:21).

There are innumerable cases on record of the fulfillment of that promise. The annals of godly families are full of instances of this spiritual succession, as the children have followed in their fathers' steps, taken up their fathers' work, preached in their pulpits, or devoted themselves to the fulfillment of their cherished ideals. God still keeps His mercy for thousands of them who love Him and keep His commandments. We do not believe that devotion is hereditary and can be passed like genius from father to child. But certainly, a predisposition to a godly life is a gracious inheritance, and in answer to believing prayer, God does, in certain families, manifestly grant a godly succession from generation to generation.

Elderly friends, pray for us. The rush and turmoil of your lives has somewhat subsided. You have crossed the stormy seas and lie safely moored in the harbor, bathed in the evening afterglow. Now lift your hearts in prayer for sons and daughters who are in their midlife years, and for the bright boys and girls who are venturing forth. Teach us the secret of the love which has blessed your days. Warn us, if we are missing the best, and call us back to the safer, better way, so a trail of light shall mark your sunset, and the heavens will be long irradiated with the beauty of the sundown.

> *Let thy work appear unto thy servants, and thy glory unto their children. And let the beauty of the Lord our God be upon us: and establish thou the work of our hands upon us; yea, the work of our hands establish thou it* (Psalm 90:16-17).

F. B. Meyer –
A Short Biography

Frederick Brotherton Meyer (1847–1929) was a Bible teacher, pastor, and evangelist of German descent, born in London. He attended Brighton College and graduated from the University of London in 1869. He studied theology at Regent's College, Oxford and went on to serve as a Baptist pastor and evangelist in England. He also devoted time to inner-city mission work in England and in America.

Meyer first became a pastor in 1870 at Pembroke Baptist Chapel in Liverpool. By 1872, he had moved on to pastor at Priory Street Baptist Church in York. It was during his tenure there that he met the well-known American evangelist Dwight L. Moody. The two of them became good friends, and the Lord used him to introduce Moody to other churches in England.

From Pembroke, he went on to pastor a number of other churches. When he accepted the pastorate at Christ Church in Lambeth in 1895, he found a meager congregation of only 100 faithful people attending, but over the next two years, God used him to breathe new life into the church and blessed him with more than 2,000 people attending on a regular basis. God planted him at Christ Church for the fifteen years, and then sent him out to preach conferences and evangelistic services. These evangelistic circuits included trips to South Africa and Asia, and even carried him across the Atlantic a number of times to the United States and Canada.

Meyer was known for his outcry against immorality and other social evils. He was part of the Higher Life Movement which was devoted to scriptural and practical Christian holiness. As a result, he tirelessly championed for the poor and needy, and his life and message were responsible for closing down more than 500 saloons and houses of prostitution. He also initiated the prison aid society. Higher Life conferences were held at Broadlands (1874), Oxford (1874), Brighton (1875), and finally at Keswick (1875). Keswick quickly became the center of the movement, which also became known as the Keswick Movement, and for many years he was closely associated with the Keswick Conferences.

During one of these conventions in 1887, as he sat listening to Hudson Taylor of the China Inland Mission speak, he suddenly realized something was missing in his life. Hudson Taylor possessed something he did not – the baptism of the Holy Spirit. That evening he walked from the Keswick tent and walked up a nearby a hill. Later he said, "I was too tired to agonize, so I left the prayer meeting and as I walked I said, 'My Father, if there is one soul more than another within the circle of these hills that needs the gift of Pentecost, it is I. I want the Holy Spirit, but I do not know how to receive Him and I am too weary to think, or feel, or pray intensively.' Then a Voice said to me, 'As you took forgiveness from the hand of the dying Christ, take the Holy Ghost from the hand of the living Christ and reckon that the gift is thine by a faith that is utterly indifferent to the presence or absence of resultant joy. According to thy faith so shall it be unto thee.' So I turned to Christ… I felt no hand laid on my head, there was no lambent flame, there was no rushing sound from heaven: but by faith without emotion, without excitement, I took, and took for the first time, and I have kept on taking ever since."[13]

This experience changed his life, and as an evangelical of singular vision, his obituary in *The Daily Telegraph* described him as the Archbishop of the Free Churches. As an author, he sold five million copies of his books during his lifetime. In all, he penned more than 40

---

13 Henry, Robert T. *The Golden Age of Preaching: Men Who Moved the Masses.* iUniverse, Lincoln Nebraska. P. 191.

books, including Christian biographies on the lives of Samuel, David, Paul, Moses, Abraham and others, as well as devotional Bible commentaries written to help Christians in their daily walk with Christ. Meyer served as President of the Free Church Council (1904), President of the World's Sunday School Association (1907), and President of the Baptist Union (1907). But with all these accomplishments Meyer made it clear that all credit went to God. He said, "I am only an ordinary man. I have no special gifts. I am no orator, no scholar, no profound thinker. If I have done anything for Christ and my generation, it is because I have given myself entirely to Christ Jesus, and then tried to do whatever He wanted me to do."

Meyer influence giants of the faith like Charles H. Spurgeon who said, "Meyer preaches as a man who has seen God face to face." In 1904-1905 he served as president of the National Federation of Free Churches; and following that term he served as an evangelist for that organization.

In his 70s, F. B. Meyer returned to the work of pastoring churches in England but still traveled to the United States and Canada. At the age of 80, he crossed the Atlantic one last time for his twelfth American preaching campaign for the Lord with a preaching style characterized as simple and direct. This campaign involved traveling more than 15,000 miles and speaking at more than 300 meetings.

He led a long and fruitful life, preaching more than 16,000 sermons before he went home to be with the Lord in 1929 at the age of 82.

Other Similar Titles

5 Things Christians Must Do,
by F. B. Meyer

This book is a refreshing, interesting, and yet challenging look at five essential aspects of healthy Christian living. These are not new, of course, as nothing can be added to what's been already recorded in scripture. Rather, the topics as they are written are a breath of fresh air in simplicity of presentation, yet striking to the core of what is necessary in order to truly follow Christ.

Available where books are sold.

Light on Life's Duties,
by F. B. Meyer

Are you prepared to sign your name to a blank sheet of paper and then hand it over to God for Him to fill in as He pleases? If not, ask Him to make you willing and able to do this and everything else. You will never be happy until you let the Lord Jesus keep the house of your nature, closely scrutinizing every visitor and admitting only His friends. He must reign. He must have all or nothing. He must have the key of every closet, of every cupboard, and of every room. Do not try to make them fit for Him. Simply give Him the key. He will cleanse and renovate and make beautiful.

Available where books are sold.

Come Ye Children,
by Charles H. Spurgeon

Teaching children things of the Lord is an honor and a high calling. Children have boundless energy and may appear distracted, but they are capable of understanding biblical truths even adults have a hard time grasping. Children's minds are easily impressed with new thoughts, whether good or bad, and will remember many of their young lessons for the rest of their life. Adults and churches tend to provide entertainment to occupy the children, but children ought to have our undivided attention. Jesus said, *let the little children come to me.* They were worthy of His time and devotion, and they are worthy of ours.

Available where books are sold.

How to Raise Children for Christ,
by Andrew Murray

This book is different from most books on raising children. It is a plea for the parents to truly know and walk with God – for them to love God and His Word. In the correct order, focusing first on the parents, Andrew Murray then urges parents to sincerely and consistently love their children and in all tenderness and gentleness teach them as God also teaches us.

Children are a most precious gift that we receive from God, and they deserve our very best. Our faithful training will not be lost on our children; this is a promise found over and over again in the Scriptures. If our hearts are right towards God and our children, the world's influence will not impact our children. We can and must exercise faith, so our children and our children's children will be able to impact the world for Christ and inherit eternal blessings.

Available where books are sold.